COACHING MINDSET

CLAIRE MOODY

A NOTE FROM THE AUTHOR

IT'S NOT ABOUT BEING THE BEST, IT'S ABOUT BEING THE BEST THAT YOU CAN BE

I wanted to write my next guidebook as I found that the first pocket guide had helped so many individuals to just stop and think about themselves. Where these days do we really stop and think about 'I' instead of 'we' or 'us'? We have one life and sometimes we get so wrapped up in what is going on around us that we never think of ourselves.

Now is your time to think about you. This mindset is key for an effective coaching culture and this guidebook will assist you in many areas where coaching skills work best. You might be a manager requiring coaching skills to develop staff, or you might just be looking for these skills to coach yourself. It doesn't matter why you have bought this book; the skills required for coaching apply to every situation. I also felt I wanted to continue the journey in developing a coaching culture using a coaching mindset and that is the purpose of this guidebook; helping people to understand what coaching actually is.

Here is the next edition, let's continue to grow together. I hope you enjoyed my first development book, but that was only the beginning so let's move forward together for the next phase. Remember: create your journey, don't let it just happen, take control. I am keen for you to buy a journal, and we will talk later about why this is important. We will also include how you can use the journal in a very effective manner to encourage change. Treat every page of this guide as a new area to reflect on and to think about yourself. Then, if you want some changes, start to make that shift. I have put together a few pages on the way a coach may think; think about yourself and use the words on yourself for reflection and change.

You may find some of the pages similar. Yes, they are, but there will be subtle differences: it is about little tweaks all the time. I have put a further reflection sheet at the end to guide you if you choose to use it. It is different from my first sheet. I have added a few more areas for you to consider, so now you have two. With reflection, don't reflect just once: continue to reflect and reflect on the reflections. This is an amazing process when done correctly, you have to be honest with yourself.

Here we go, let's begin our work together

Claire Moody

Claire Moody

targettrg.co.uk

ARE YOU COACHABLE?

I recently had a bit of a lightbulb moment when I heard someone say that they ask their people if they are coachable. I noticed in myself that I stopped for a second to think about what I had just heard. I could not really articulate the feeling that appeared in me, to hear "Are you coachable?" I was amazed that someone would even ask someone else if they thought they were coachable. And then ask them to fill in a form!!! I was genuinely really shocked at this statement.

Why would they not be coachable? Surely everyone is coachable? Imagine choosing who you think is coachable, what does this say about you? What sort of judgements are coming from you? How you make your decision on who you think is coachable is based on your interpretation of the world; that is not the way to be.

We can all be coached in any area of our life. Choose one area to start with, and then get going. I think you have to remember that coaching is a development and it usually takes place between two people. The two people work together to change past patterns; that is, if the coachee desires change.

Everyone wants to change if they are honest with themselves. It is very easy to push to the back of their mind areas they don' t want to face. I think the key is to recognise you are doing this, then think about why, and what you would like to be different. Coaching requires energy, commitment and work to change patterns. Everyone can be coached once they understand what coaching means. The world of possibilities is there for everyone.

Coaching is fantastic and can create so much improvement in yourself and others, creating self-motivation and positivity which helps individuals both personally and professionally. It is a habit that needs to be built so your brain always follows that pathway. Understanding coaching is really important, so what is it? What can it do, and what takes place in a coaching session? You are coachable; everyone is, if they would like to be.

Follow this guide and you will start to realise you can change and be coached on any area you would like. I have taken some areas I think about as a coach and I use them in this guide to help you think about how coaches may think or observe. Incredibly powerful techniques to use and think about. Let's move forward, recognising you can be coached. Coach yourself following this pocket guide. Let's get some change in our lives. Small changes lead to big improvements, so let's begin.

As mentioned in my first guide, my mantra is " It' s not about being the best, it's about being the best you can be", and this guide continues to provide you with the understanding to apply this philosophy accordingly.

ARE YOU COACHABLE? YES
DO YOU WANT CHANGE? YES

CONTENTS

Coaching - why it continues to grow 7

Do you ever feel you're going to be found out? 10

What's going on in your own head? 14

What do you notice when you feel irritated? 18

What do you notice when someone enters a room? 21

Do you notice the dance that happens when people meet? 24

What do the first twenty minutes look like for you at work? 27

Have you ever walked away from a meeting thinking... 31

Ask yourself the question, are you present in a conversation? 35

Staying silent in a conversation, silence is golden. 38

Do you need a conclusion in a conversation? 42

Is there something about you that invites someone in? 44

It is all data in the room. 48

How do you prepare? 52

What do you notice when someone asks you for a meeting? 56

Create the same awareness as the person entering the room. 60

The problem with being too organised. 64

Why everyone needs coaching skills. 67

There is always time in the year to make changes, it doesn't... 71

Reflection sheet - Questions. 75

Coaching - Why it
Continues to Grow

SECTION 1

I still like Timothy Gallwey's statement on performance coaching. He said the worst opponent is in your head; this is so true. The most critical person about your own performance will be you and most of it will be self- created by your own inner voice, the voice that only you hear and listen to, the inner critic.

Coaching provides techniques to take away the barriers that are in coachees' heads. Work is like sport; it is about managing what goes on in the head. Tim Gallwey also said, "Fighting the mind does not work, what works best is learning to focus it." Coaching provides the focus in a safe environment where changes can take place. Coaching can give an increased awareness to the coachee from the coach by simply guiding around the data that presents itself in the room. Performance coaching will drive coachees using simple techniques like GROW, Relational/ Gestalt coaching will look at all of the data in the room; the feelings and instincts that pop up. The balance is the use of both to develop the coachee. So, develop yourself, think about what you notice. For the coach, the question has to be how to deliver good questions in such a way as to help the coachee's natural learning process and not interfere with it. Question Technique is crucial to a good coaching session. Guiding, not telling, is the key as this gives the coachee the time to focus on any area they wish to. All the coach is doing is directing or guiding the thinking; the coach is not doing the thinking, the coachee is. The coach is allowing this to happen.

The only open question I think about using less than others is the use of "Why". This is because it takes the coachee to the analytical process in their brain and may be negative. You must be very skilled to know when to use this. To develop into a great coach you require practice; coaching is all about increasing awareness and this is why it continues to grow.

It is fantastic in the workplace and in improving performance in individuals, which in turn improves performance in the business they are employed in. Invest in people and they will grow the business, not the other way round. Think about the questions I pose you through this guidebook, really think about you and don't let the inner critic win. It is probably talking to you now, take control and focus it in a more positive way. The inner critic is always negative. It will always tell you that you are not good enough and will stop you making change; don't let it.

Do you ever feel you are
going to be found out?

SECTION
2

targettrg.co.uk | © 2020 ClaireMoody

Within my coaching practice I have heard recurring patterns in the language that is used by coachees who enter the room. Here is a question to the reader: have you ever heard yourself saying or thinking "It was an easy task", or discounting praise when it has been given to you, saying something like "I'm just doing my job"? It is so interesting hearing or thinking "I feel like a phoney" or "am I good enough to do this job?" I have heard comments like this from barristers, surgeons, healthcare assistants and individuals of all ranks in the armed forces with different skill sets from pilots to infantry soldiers.

Amazing how many of us carry this, quite fascinating. Lots of people feel this, they feel they are hiding something. They feel they are not capable to be in the position they find themselves in, a feeling of are they good enough to be doing the task. The "imposter syndrome" is what it is called, and it is everywhere. In fact, through life 70 % of us will feel this at some point, some more than others. It may come when you compare yourself to someone else, maybe when you have started a new job, for example. Basically, it's a feeling of being inadequate. Sometimes this will be unbalanced because you may not like to recognise your accomplishments, the fact you are even there.

We all compare ourselves, but we don't always compare ourselves in a balanced way, usually failing to look at the positives as well. Sadly, this can be aggravated by the 'be perfect' driver or if you have low self- esteem. But why? Where does this come from? In some of us it may be because when we were young someone in authority said something like, "You're not good enough to do that job" or "That is not for people like us". Fascinating to consider this from your own personal level. The coaching room is a safe place to discuss this.

It is away from peers, family and friends, with someone who is objective and ready to listen to your own feelings and thoughts and look at your own behaviours. Create your own coaching room, somewhere you can go and think about you and where you come from. Use the journal I would encourage you to buy as mentioned in my first pocket guide. If you wish to change any part of your imposter syndrome, the key is to focus on the positives.

Look at your comments through the day and reflect on the language you use. Do you have the imposter syndrome, how much and why? Great reflection in YOU can create massive changes, a very powerful tool for change when it is done properly. Sadly, not many people know how to reflect correctly and unbalanced thinking hurts confidence and stops personal progress.

What does your imposter stop you doing?

Write down what you believe happens when your imposter takes hold:

What is going on in your own head?

SECTION 3

SECTION THREE

In the first two sections I mentioned the imposter syndrome and the inner critic. They play a massive part in your head, but they can be changed. Our heads are full of habits and patterns, this is where we are most comfortable.

How difficult is it to create new habits? It is sometimes very hard, so we choose not to do it? Pushing yourself to step out of your comfort zone is hard, forcing a new habit is hard, but you can always do it if you choose to do it and focus.

Sometimes a coach can create that change for you by guiding a new habit, a change in the way that you think. As human beings, we are very set in our ways and the brain does not like change unless we force that habit in. The key is to create a habit of enjoying change. What an amazing change in the way you can think if you choose to. We very often tell ourselves we can't do things, sometimes the way to deal with that is to do first what you fear most. Force that habit in, the tasks of the day. We tend to leave the ones we don't want to do until later, how about doing them first? Enjoy the feeling of completeness and the fact you dealt with it, force this new habit in yourself. This is just a suggestion, there are plenty more that may appeal to you.

You can conquer anything if you choose to do it, but really think about you, where you are and what you notice in yourself. What do you do, have you ever reflected on your habits? Have you really looked at your habits? Such patterns that can recur in life, throughout your life.

Remember you don't have to stay with them, you can change them if you decide to do this, then act on your decision to change your habit.

Habits are great, but create great ones, get rid of those you don't like about yourself and create a change. When you recognise you are about to do something that is an old habit, then stop and think about your decision, you have a choice. If you focus on this, you can notice this moment in yourself. The choice to change the direction or the choice to stay the same, what do you want? The more difficult choice, although wanting it, will be changing the direction of travel. However, once the choice has been made a few times, you can slowly change that habit. It works, try it. Keep a record at the end of the day, see what choices have come up and the directions you have chosen.

Write down a new habit you would like to make

A useful exercise to see what you think you have done, to see what you really have done. Start somewhere though, begin today. Pick up the journal.

I feel some motivation in you, that is great – stay motivated. Motivation is great for beginning the change and new habits, but the motivation will slow down. The key is getting the habit in before your motivation dries up. Use your journal, start writing down at the end of the day any small improvements you have made. It only needs to take five minutes. Don't make it a pain, so you don't stay with it. Small changes, remember, are the key to success in your life.

Write down the key things that motivate you

What do you notice when you feel irritated?

SECTION 4

Have you ever noticed the direction you choose when you get irritated? The build- up, do you recognise what is happening in you? I always feel the tension in me when I start to get irritated, I look for when it starts to build. You have to ask yourself what triggers this.

As you coach yourself, think about the word irritation, what does this mean for you? We all have levels of irritability, but I think it is a good awareness to know where your level is and what you notice in you. As you try to change something in your life, you will get irritated with yourself. This is OK, just recognise this.

Sometimes it may be your values, you feel your values are being eroded. Sometimes your beliefs may be questioned, which annoys you. I think it is great watching people start to get irritated. The speed of their response to people when they question back or respond seems to change when they feel they are being challenged. It may be work pressure that triggers people or lack of time they have to deal with all the inputs placed on them. Life sometimes is not easy.

What can you do when the irritation starts to happen? What do you recognise in yourself when you start to feel irritated, and why? Watch the change in a room when someone gets irritated with someone else, what happens to you? What do you notice in your changes even as an observer? Do you feel the tension? If so, where? You can guarantee you will feel something, but what? And how do you respond to this? Do you stay calm or do you feel that you need to intervene?

If your trigger is to stay calm, why do you do this? What does calmness mean to you? If your trigger is to get involved, why is this?

Always reflect to learn. Start to use your journal in this area. Have a look, I think it is a great area to notice in yourself. It's really interesting to notice 'You' in any situation, whether you get irritated or you watch someone else get irritated. Next time focus on you, your feelings, your thoughts and your behaviours, what changes?

A great experience for you to think about with just this one tiny area that affects everyone. I think you can never stop learning about yourself, and to be at your best you have to understand yourself really well.

That state of feeling that you get annoyed, irritated, impatient or slightly angry, these can all take you of course. If it becomes a problem for you, you can change it. You can change anything in life if you choose to, just sit with that one for a moment. And on that point, what have you thought about, what have you noticed in you, any feelings or thoughts? If so, reflect and if there is nothing, reflect on that. There is always something to notice as you continue to grow in your life. Regardless of age, you are constantly learning: lifelong learning. I felt this area was a good place to start reflecting on some personality areas of yourself. That fuse that people have, how much does it take to make you irritable or irritated with yourself, and why? What was it? Remember to write things down then constantly reflect.

What do you notice when someone enters a room?

SECTION 5

I find it interesting watching how someone enters a room. Before any coaching session, I always take five minutes to relax, slow down and just sit in a room. This allows me to watch who enters the room and how they enter. How can I be fully present if I don't do this and how can I clear all judgements I have otherwise? My day may have created some changes in me, so I must be disciplined to be in control of myself and park everything to one side.

I think those first few seconds tell you so much about what is about to open up. The words come but you will notice so much more if you think about what you notice and sense, and if any behaviours appear in you or the client. Think about you and how you enter a room. What changes you, and what various moods change the way you enter? As you enter this changes the dynamics in the room, an important area to reflect on.

Think about it, someone may enter in a rush; a huge presence, how does that make you feel? How do you react? If you're not fully aware and conscious of yourself you will feel the transference and start rushing too. It's really interesting to be fully present to understand what data you are witnessing. You really must concentrate on this process, what do you notice in both the client and you? So, for you, what do you notice about you?

What if someone enters all bubbly with words but you notice something different about them? When you start coaching, it can be useful to share this.

Remember everything you notice and feel, and any behaviours are all data. The body's reactions, how someone sits down, how someone moves. How much they talk and how much they are looking at you for answers, so many key things happening in front of you and the key is to catch them.

What do you notice about you, what are you not admitting to yourself, and what is not being said? The key is to attack what you are noticing and say it out aloud. This can create changes. Remember, small changes are fantastic, they work. It really is essential to be fully present with anyone. To achieve this, you must be very well trained to notice everything in the room.

Coaching is not about question technique. It is about, at the point of asking your next question, sharing something you notice. This can be such a critical moment in coaching. Critical moments can create a real paradigm and lightbulb moment. When you are coaching yourself, be present – it is the best you can be.

Really think about what happens when you enter a room, think about you and others and what do you notice

YOU	OTHERS

Do you notice the dance that happens when people meet?

SECTION 6

SECTION SIX

What happens when you meet someone, how does the rapport build, what do you actually do?

I am constantly amused by those first few moments in a meeting, whether it is with a person walking into an office, or by Skype, etc. Think about you, what do you do? Really notice your movements, your introductions. Is this the start of the rapport building, basically you putting someone at ease, or is it for you as you adjust yourself? Think about what the first impressions are that you receive from the coachee. How does this change your questioning? Remember, it can create your judgements in those first few seconds. How do you meet people? On Skype or Zoom, I love little jiggles as screens are adjusted left or right, the nervous giggles, or slightly uncomfortable feeling, the anticipation. I personally enjoy these moments; I gain a lot in my coaching from the first couple of minutes. What do I notice, what do I sense, what is my instinct telling me, what thoughts are then created and what are the behaviours that follow?

I think it is great to reflect and ask yourself, who is this for? Do you need to do this? Have you created a pattern or a habit, so you do it every time? Reflection on the first few moments can be incredibly powerful. Really notice this at your next meeting, regardless of whom it is with. It' s really fascinating, as you build your notes, to ask yourself who this is for and start to write down those first few minutes. Your journal must be growing brilliantly at the moment, constantly looking at yourself, well done.

Then look at any trends that have developed, do you always do the same? Are you stuck? Are you fully aware or are you going through the motions really settling yourself? These are always good questions to ask yourself and reflect on. You may find patterns between the different characters or ages. It's hugely interesting to watch how you respond during those first few minutes. I know my patterns. I know what may appear if I let it control me, so I sit, watch and notice what happens in front of me and my instinct really tells me a lot.

I have learnt to pay attention to me. Coaching yourself, when learnt correctly, is just the most amazing skill set to be able to use.

You will find it is helpful to use tools and techniques, but it is not about a bag of techniques. Rather, it is about really noticing and looking at yourself as you enter into a relationship.

Watch that dance, it's hugely interesting and tells you a lot about yourself. It's important to notice the ages, gender and labels people carry; these can make you change. This really tells you a lot about yourself.

What do the first twenty
minutes look like for you
at work?

SECTION 7

SECTION SEVEN

WHAT DO THE FIRST TWENTY MINUTES LOOK LIKE FOR YOU AT WORK?

Please read below a short page I wrote on myself one morning, then think about yourself and how you are energised in the mornings. This is such a fantastic area to reflect on, what do your first twenty minutes look like at work or anywhere else?

I begin: "I feel tired this morning sitting at my desk, sitting with a cup of coffee to wake me up. We have all been there, it is Thursday. The week is moving forward towards the weekend, every day for me has a different feeling. What makes my first few minutes tick, I ponder, and decide to notice as I sit here after arriving first in the office. What do I recognise and feel as I sit and what makes me start to energise? I start to feel a rise and being slightly energised by the radio in the corner of the room. Switching it on is the first thing I do as I enter the room. I start to type this thinking about the energy starting to rise in me. I thought I would follow and write what I am feeling and noticing in myself. A fellow office worker arrives, and a relationship starts: "Morning", "How are you?", "What did you do last night?" - general chit chat. But I notice my energy levels rising slightly further. I continue to chat, and we share a discussion on something we had just heard on the radio. Now I notice my energy levels are around 5 out of 10 instead of 3 out of 10. It's interesting to monitor yourself and recognise what is going on in you and how you change through the first few minutes of your day. What happens next is that I pick up my mobile phone, check the texts that have popped up, and notice I feel more energised as the texts appear. I feel more responsive. I really notice my energy levels rising."

"I really notice I like the interruptions. My energy continues to rise with them, the mobile phone is a good interruption. The phone on my desk starts to ring. I start to be even more responsive with further interruptions. I really like this and respond. "

It is great to reflect and to think about you. I would suggest starting to write in your journal about your mornings, noticing patterns.

I think it is interesting to monitor yourself and your own energy levels and how you change with the interruptions that appear.

I continue:

"My energy levels are now around 6 or 7. How interesting, I feel more productive now, my extraversion preference being fed. This may not be the same for you. In fact, you may be the opposite: the more interruptions, the lower your energy drops.

As others turn up, I find my energy levels rising even further. I really notice, over the last twenty minutes, how much I have changed. I know if I had not had the interruptions my energy levels would have stayed a lot lower. That is my preference. I respond to everything around me. But what if I didn't, what if I had more of an introverted preference? How many of those interruptions would have felt intrusive, unnecessary, getting in the way of my internal energy, a very different feeling?"

Really notice in yourself how your energy levels are fed and how the opposite preference in the individuals around you may be feeling.

There is no right way to be, just notice what affects you, but be respectful of others and be aware not everyone is the same.

This is just an example of me, with a layer of reflection looking at my extraversion preference. I do reflect a lot deeper than this, but initially this is how to start. Think of yourself and what you are noticing, where does your preference lie? A great exercise to understand something about you. Extraversion and Introversion are so different and probably one of the big misunderstandings that people have. Extraversion does not mean being gregarious, and introversion does not mean shyness: they are basically how we are energised.

Have you ever walked away from a meeting thinking you have agreed on something, then what you haven't agreed starts to happen?

SECTION 8

SECTION EIGHT

HAVE YOU EVER WALKED AWAY FROM A MEETING THINKING YOU HAVE AGREED ON SOMETHING, THEN WHAT YOU HAVEN'T AGREED STARTS TO HAPPEN?

This is all about how we take in our information, we are so different. Some of us really like facts, really enjoy facts and actually need them to hang on to. Then there are others who find facts restrict their thinking. The facts get in the way, they can see better ways of doing things. Some people like facts for evidence, others don't. Ask yourself a couple of questions, 'Do you rely on facts?' or 'Do you think in a more creative way?' Yes, you will do both, but what do you do first, where do you go when you take on a task?

A useful exercise in understanding yourself and why you may clash with others is to actually work out what your preference may be. Look at a picture and think about what you see first: colours, shapes, pictures? Or do you go straight to the artist, or ask if it is oil based, or put a bigger picture onto what you see? This is a great exercise to see how different people around you are and what they see. No one way is the right way and you don't want everyone to be the same, organisations need the mix.

However, you need to be aware of how it can come across. I recently had some time with a very bright young man, clearly an Oxbridge individual with the way he thought outside the box on everything. It was great to work with him. I suggested he might need to be careful because some people around him would not always follow his thinking and would find him very vague and hard to understand. He had no idea and was shocked when, with a few simple exercises, he realised how differently people think.

SECTION EIGHT

HAVE YOU EVER WALKED AWAY FROM A MEETING THINKING YOU HAVE AGREED ON SOMETHING, THEN WHAT YOU HAVEN'T AGREED STARTS TO HAPPEN?

He had a lightbulb moment when we were discussing this. He realised that this was probably why people did not always do what he thought they had agreed on. "How fascinating", he said, that is why some people appear negative to him, he actually said this. Some of his colleagues are likely to be practical, to like experience, and are probably very matter- of- fact. This is what may appear negative to a creative type, because factual people can't see all the creative ideas working.

The skill is to have everyone working together and the practical people following up on the creative ideas, well the realistic ones, the ones the factual people can see working.

When have you experienced this issue, could be at work or at home

SECTION EIGHT

HAVE YOU EVER WALKED AWAY FROM A MEETING THINKING YOU HAVE AGREED ON SOMETHING, THEN WHAT YOU HAVEN'T AGREED STARTS TO HAPPEN?

The key message to understand from this page is how differently we take in our information and how frustrated we can be within our workplace where we see negativity, creativity, vagueness and lack of direction. Remember, people will see things very differently. Ask yourself, how do I take my information in, how am I seen by others?

PRACTICAL:	CREATIVE:
• ENJOY PRACTICAL CONVERSATIONS	• ENJOY CLEVER CONVERSATIONS
• MOVE FROM POINT TO POINT	• SKIP AROUND IN CONVERSATIONS
• USE DETAILED DESCRIPTIONS	• USE METAPHORICAL DESCRIPTIONS
• ENHANCE MESSAGES USING EXPERIENCE	• ENHANCE MESSAGES USING IMAGINATION

Ask yourself the question, are you present in a conversation?

SECTION 9

SECTION NINE

ASK YOURSELF THE QUESTION, ARE YOU PRESENT IN A CONVERSATION?

"Are you fully present?" is a funny question and if you ask someone who has not really done any coaching they will say 'yes' and not think much more about it. So, my question to you is to reflect on what it means to be fully present.

Think about it, where is your focus when someone is speaking to you? Where are your thoughts and feelings, where are you focused? Have you ever asked yourself and reflected on this after a conversation? Most people in a conversation will be thinking about their next question, and the next question may stem from their own judgement. It's really interesting to observe this. It is vital to be aware that some of your questions may come from your own biases and judgements.

Have you ever reflected on this after a conversation? I mean, really reflected on your patterns? I think in any conversation it is vital to be fully focused on the here and now, to have a full awareness of the conversation taking place. It is important to park any ideas or judgements, and just listen. Awareness is central to a conversation; it is so much more important that you notice what is happening with your thoughts and feelings in a conversation.

We tend in our busy lives to think about the next five minutes or the past five minutes, the past or future is where we spend most of our time. We never train ourselves to think about the present, we rarely think about the here and now. People are much more aware these days of the here and now. But how many of us actually practise this? The key is to create a new habit.

It is important to have a mindful conversation to separate your thoughts and feelings and what is

SECTION NINE

ASK YOURSELF THE QUESTION, ARE YOU PRESENT IN A CONVERSATION?

happening in you. Whether you manage, coach or train as a profession, or whether you are just talking to friends and family, either way it is extremely important that you listen in a conversation.

The way I do this is to sit for a few minutes in silence and notice what is coming up for me, if I can. This is by far the best way to start to feel present. Being present in a room is important before a conversation takes place.

It is hugely important to build this as a habit before you sit with anyone. Obviously, you cannot always do this but, if you can, have a go, watch the differences in you. When I was first introduced to being present, I was not sure of it, I was a little bit sceptical. But after I made it a habit and started to recognise what the words 'being present' meant, I embraced it and really " got" it. But moreover, I understood how important it is and how useful to create change for anyone you are talking to, and for yourself.

So, journal. Here we go, that journal should be filling up. I suggest you start to reflect on your writing. If you still haven't bought yourself a new "me journal", there is still time. As I have said before, make it special, important to you. People sometimes say "journal, why bother, what is the point?" The problem is you will miss things and when you start to see how your writing builds, other areas you could change start to pop out. Journaling really is a very powerful tool for change. I cannot recommend it enough. But always write positives down, balance out the writing, what are you happy and grateful for? Every day write this. The last thing you want is a journal full of negatives.

Staying silent in a conversation, silence is golden

SECTION 10

Coaching is an amazing process to help individuals to improve in any area of their life, both professionally and personally. Since mastering my coaching skills, I have found that staying silent can be an incredible experience. I genuinely love to see the change in individuals by asking the miracle question, this only happens if you stay silent and notice. Start to think about what you do. When you have a conversation and watch the other person, firstly try to feel what it is like sitting in their shoes. You must genuinely watch and really notice and listen. If you listen with the intention to fully understand rather than the intention to reply with your next question, you will notice so much more. If you interrupt, you will be planting a suggestion or judgement based on your interpretation of the situation. It really is important to listen so as to fully understand. This silence will direct you to an open question, but only if you allow it to happen.

Remember, as a coach you question to guide the coachee, not to offer a solution. To really begin to understand this process, you need to gain experience. Its not done overnight; this skill takes time. So, think about you and developing yourself in a conversation. Silence is golden and incredibly hard to sit with, especially if you have the extraverted preference. It is a discipline that needs to be trained and is incredibly hard to do well. If someone is talking, people sometimes think, how long before I intervene? Or they just jump in with their own judgement; the key is not to. Someone may talk for up to ten minutes, but whether it is one minute or ten, most people will find themselves drawn in.

However, it is essential as a coach that you stay silent so, for you, think about how long you stay silent. Then when the natural silence appears you can offer what you have noticed, felt or heard. This can be incredibly powerful; the other person tends to have an amazing reaction if you share rather than tell them what to do. The following are key: ·

- You will get a completely different reaction than if you had stepped in and interrupted the flow with your own judgement. Focus on what they are saying, not what your response is going to be or your next question.

- Summarise what they say to check you have understood. Everyone's interpretations are different, we all take in our information differently.

- Listen to what words keep coming up and what they are not saying. Coaching is all about what is not being said. It is great to understand this so you can develop yourself.

Silence is key. Bite your tongue, don't judge, just listen. The relationship is always so much better this way.

Back to the journal. Watch yourself as you sit in silence. For some of us it is an uncomfortable time, for others energising. But be disciplined to sit and notice, then write. This is another powerful technique to master. Try it and watch how you grow once you realise what you do.

Do you need a conclusion in a conversation?

SECTION 11

Have you ever left a meeting or even a training session and thought, I'm not sure how useful that was? Have you ever left a relationship feeling, I'm not sure what just happened was any good? Ask yourself how you feel after any form of meeting. Do you feel you need to have a conclusion? Do you feel that there must be an ending, or maybe not? I find it very interesting that some people do like endings.

People generally like something to cling on to, a solution. It helps them think that what has just happened had a purpose. Have you ever thought, who is that for? Do you like endings, a solution, and drive the session to get a result?

There are preferences in everyone: some like endings, some don't. In a simple conversation, it is always interesting to register what is going for you, then think about whether the ending is for you or the other person. I find it very useful to notice in me and to recognise what I find important. The key is to be able to put that to one side and be open. The other person may not need a solution. They may just want a conversation where they have something small to work on or to talk about. This does not need to have an ending after an hour's conversation. I would suggest it is a good idea to look at yourself and what you recognise in how you feel after a meeting. Really focus on whether you may have driven the conversation for your own benefit, to get a solution for you, to make you feel good. I would start reflecting on this area, as it can be very useful to recognise your feelings and patterns. Coaching when done well is fantastic for self- awareness.

SECTION ELEVEN

DO YOU NEED A CONCLUSION IN A CONVERSATION?

Most people don't pay attention to what is really going on in a conversation, they just listen to the words. Language is only 7 % of communication, yet the majority of people focus on this. The instincts just sit without attention being paid to them. Some people in life like routine, conclusions, planning – but some don't. Some prefer casual spontaneity and endings left open. Where are you on this? What do you prefer? Look at yourself and ask how planned your day is, compared to if you leave it to see what pops up. There are big differences between people. Obviously, this area goes far deeper than the few words I have just put down for you to think about. But what is your preference and how do you drive your way in conversations? I think this is a great question to leave 'you' the reader to reflect on.

Is there something about
you that invites someone in?

SECTION
12

Do you ever think why an individual has approached you, is it out of choice or has someone suggested they talk to you? Some people may have advised it may be a good idea to talk to you. What is it about you that the individual feels comfortable with? In life we tend to spend most time with people most like ourselves. Your friends will be people that are most like you, it is a natural choice. I think it is interesting to spend time with people who are not like you, to develop and understand further. Step out of your comfort zone to grow.

When someone does approach you, chances are that they are like you. But if someone has suggested they talk to you, then they may not be like you. This may result in you not enjoying the conversation as much. You may feel slightly uncomfortable. If you are uncomfortable, do you change the way you are with them? Do you hold yourself back when talking? Do you advise, question in a different way, a more judgemental way? Are the conversations shorter because you are uncomfortable with them? It is really interesting to notice in you how you are in certain conversations. Use that wonderful Journal, create a chapter just for this. You will start to notice the differences if you pay attention to this. This is a really useful exercise in developing yourself. What do you feel in different conversations, with people like you and people not like you, what don't you enjoy? Are there values that are different or is it your beliefs that may be different (values and beliefs are not the same)? Or is it something as simple as basic preferences (extraversion/introversion) or the way people make decisions – empathetically or objectively, task-focused or relationship-focused?

All of this creates changes in you when talking to someone. I would seriously start to notice this, as it can be a great area to improve in yourself, whether in a professional or personal setting. In life there are times when we feel very drained in a conversation, notice why.

Are you more drained in a relationship conversation or in a task- focused conversation? Really look at you when faced with this and ask when or if you cut conversations short.

This is a great self- reflection area, really be self-critical to understand yourself. It's vital to notice this as you need to understand what people may see in you. What you think may be shown, may be what is not seen? How we think we come across may not be how we actually do come across.

Really pay attention to any thoughts that may pop up or any feelings that appear and ask yourself what is going on for you.

Enjoy reflecting and journaling. I would imagine if you have been following this guidebook effectively there will be some areas to really reflect on in your journal.

Write down what you notice in yourself when you meet people?

It is all data in the room

SECTION 13

When you are with someone, the key is to notice what is happening in yourself and the other person or, in my case, in my coachee. Everything you feel in the room is data, instinct. Always think what is missing, what am I not saying, what is the other person not saying? What is not being said?

Then think about sharing this. Sometimes it is about taking a risk, but it is how you get it across that counts, so no one is offended.

People believe it is all about question technique in a conversation that wins, I agree. That said, it must be balanced with all the other data around you. So many times in Supervision/Coaching I witness people thinking about good question technique, thinking about how to ask the next open question. This is hard to master, but the harder act to master is to not ask the question, but to notice. At the point of asking the next question, think about sharing something you notice rather than asking the question. The timing of this is also a key skill to learn and master. But try it, notice if there is a shift in you or the other person.

Listening and sharing are great coaching skills and can be an added skill to enhance great training skills.

Training and coaching as always get mixed up and boundaries get crossed. Coaching can sometimes get fantastic results and can be amazing with just three or four questions. The killer question can be the critical moment that comes from watching, noticing, feeling and behaviours being shared.

I think sometimes we feel something but seem afraid to say it for fear of getting a reaction or hurting someone's feelings. But the key is how to say it. Something as simple as "If you don't mind, something has come up for me. Would you mind if I share this?" or "I am noticing something, do you mind if I say/ share it?", whatever 'it' is. This way you are setting the person up for something, almost asking their permission. This way the person cannot come back with anything. Usually you will see a reaction. Look for this and then share that. For example, "I noticed on that comment a second's delay in your reaction" or "you sat back slightly or appeared to look more thoughtful", what could this mean? This can be an amazing situation, creating lightbulb moments in coaching and some change for someone.

This is a great coaching skill which is fantastic and when individuals understand the differences between training and coaching, they really will know when to use this skill. I hear so many times, once people understand, that training and coaching are so different. Delegates often say, "I never realised the differences before". There are always lightbulb moments. Start to think about the data you notice, and as you get used to doing this and making notes on what you notice, you will grow.

When have you ever not said what you should have said in a meeting? Start to make notes on what you notice in yourself.

How do you prepare?

SECTION 14

What is preparation? We all in our busy lives tend to rush through the day, not always giving ourselves time to prepare thoroughly. Whether it is for coaching, training, management or coffee with a friend. Which brings me into asking 'you' to think about how you prepare. What do you actually do regardless of the type of meeting?

In my coaching practice I have found through experience that the best way to prepare is to sit for ten minutes before a coachee enters the room. In those minutes, "To be the best you can be for the coachee", you need to separate any judgements, any thoughts you may have already subconsciously made and what you may be carrying from both your professional and personal life. You may have had a busy morning; you may wear two hats! Two very different roles that you may have to separate. A really fantastic way to be prepared for the coachee is to bring 'you' into the present just by sitting. If you don't do this, even the questions you may pose will be judgemental, you may create questions that fit what you have subconsciously thought about. Looking to question and not listen.

Those ten minutes can be exceptional when done correctly and make the difference. What do you do when you sit for those ten minutes? Think about what you are noticing about yourself, what you are feeling, sensing and thinking, how is your breathing, really focus. It is remarkable that if you build in a routine like this you will notice, see and hear so much more.

You may notice sounds that have always been there but you paid little attention to. You may notice the position of the chairs in the room, the way the wind is blowing outside, the smells in the room. Think about what a coachee may notice as they enter the room. We all live our lives so fast, we are always thinking about what we have just done or where we are going next, never what we are experiencing in the here and now, the present.

These ten minutes can create a perfect space for the coachee to enter the room. The relaxed atmosphere created helps the coachee settle down. You will notice so much more in the person, your awareness will be so much better when they enter and sit with you. Think about the coachee when they sit down. Really think about them and how they may be feeling when they enter, notice them. Enter the room yourself and sit in the coachees chair and notice what they will see.

It is an amazing feeling to get rid of any thoughts beforehand, those ten minutes really count. You are so much more prepared to just watch and listen to the coachee to fully understand them. You can really feel the coachee more if you share what you are sensing, feeling and noticing with them. First, though, you have to bring yourself into the present to increase your awareness. Next time you are preparing, try this. See how you get on and then reflect afterwards. It is a very powerful technique once learnt. Always make the time, create the habit, because it works fantastically well.

How are you going to prepare for your next meeting with someone?

What do you notice when someone asks you for a meeting?

SECTION 15

I think in life with any form of meeting we do not always notice the approach of an individual. For me, it is when someone asks for a coaching session. The lack of eye contact, the feeling of being tense, embarrassed and unsure of what may come, I can see it and sense it. The positive is that the individual has asked and is prepared to make a change in their life, the time is obviously going to be important to them.

It is important to think about the individuals who approach you, what they may be thinking. They will make a judgement on your reactions and what they notice in you. If you spend a few seconds watching the person, just think what they may be noticing about you. They may feel you have a sense of authority and they may be nervous in how they think you may be thinking about them. Who knows? Never assume.

I really feel it is important to pay close attention to your own reaction when you are asked for a meeting (or, in my case, coaching) and the signals that you may show. Those first signals can send a message, then a judgement may be created by the individual. Mixed messages can come from a glance or a few seconds' hesitation because you were unprepared for the individual who has asked. So much can come from those few seconds. It's vitally important to be disciplined with your reactions. Have you ever been in a situation where someone planned to meet you but never turned up? Sometimes this may happen, the problem is most people aren't aware of how important those few seconds may be.

What is the right reaction? Is there a right reaction? The key is to show huge interest in making the person feel important and, moreover, to show that whatever the person has to say is also important to you. If it is important to them then it is to you, so you can fully understand. This can create a solid rapport to start with and a relaxed feeling between the pair of you. Be careful when the person talks in case something may trigger in you, a link from the conversation to your own thoughts, feelings and behaviours. You must stay disciplined and very aware of what is going on between you. You have to recognise and park your judgements. This is well worth reflecting on as there may be a pattern in you.

It is really important your self- awareness is strong in this process; you will be able to spot patterns in yourself if you reflect. In your own reflection, make notes in your journals as to how you respond, there will be lots more going on. Remember, 55 % of communication is instinct, not what is being said, not words, words are 7 %. We must be disciplined and ask ourselves what is really going on for me?

Yet another great skill to master. You will be developing exceptionally well now with some of the pages in this guidebook. Go over and over again on the pages, see what jumps out with your thoughts. Watch that inner critic taking control; it will do, and it will be negative. Stop it, focus it for changes in your life.

How do you feel when someone asks you for a meeting?

Create the same awareness as the person entering the room

SECTION 16

This is a skill I have learnt as it is hugely important in any form of meeting. The aim is to have the awareness of the person who enters the room. I have mentioned the room a number of times in this guidebook, because It is hugely important to understand.

In my practice, I always encourage coaches to feel what it is like sitting in the coachees' shoes, to really understand where they may be. How do you do this?

I have built an amazing pattern in my coaching life to begin this process so that I really understand how the coachee may be feeling. A question for you 'the reader': when was the last time you sat in your room but in the opposite chair? What an amazing experience this is. I encourage all the coaches who attend my courses to do this. If you do, you will recognise and see what the coachee may see when they are faced with your chair and you. This will increase your awareness to a higher level.

You may be shocked with this experience, most people are, if you enter the room and just sit in the other chair for five minutes. When you do this, you can really focus on what is around you, you can imagine and sense the coachee's feelings. Really notice what they may see, the pictures and posters that surround you, really notice the smell, and what all of this may say to them. That sense of authority that may be there, the anxiety being in the room, what their feelings will be. Think about how you feel when faced with this situation and how you feel when you are anxious. Really notice how this experiment makes you feel. The patterns when people are faced with adversity are so different.

As a coach I really focus on the importance of this: you will feel so much more about the person who enters. It creates space to observe, the most important part of coaching. Remember, coaching is all about what is not being said and it really begins even before the coachee enters the room. So, for you, whichever chair you sit in, consider this. Consider the room and what may be seen.

This is another powerful technique to experience and build, and amazing for your own personal development. Whether you are thinking professionally or personally, awareness is so important and sometimes things that seem so simple are missed.

When I meet anyone I always focus and observe what is going on, I really focus on sitting in the other person's shoes. This is an amazing reflection area, the room. We are all busy but sometimes forget what areas are important, we all tend to focus on fixing a solution.

How could you improve in the area of being aware?

The problem with being too organised

SECTION 17

Work – regardless of where you work – tends to condition us on processes and tasks at the expense of human relationships. This stops us from noticing and listening. We tend to be so conditioned that we can over- prepare and create judgements on what we think we are going to get when speaking to someone. The problem with this is we will question based on our judgements, so driving the conversation to suit us if we are in the lead. A common fault with the person who sits in the authority seat if they are unaware.

How often do we notice body language in a room? Being organised stops us noticing what appears in front of us. You have to be organised to be there in the first place, but the key to really know what is presenting itself to you is to pay attention to what comes up, really watching. If someone mentions their dad three times or moves their body in a different way when mentioning something, how often do we share this? Sometimes there is a lightbulb moment, a real wow moment if shared, and this can create a change in the conversation, take it to another level. It shows you are actively listening and empathising, which can change the relationship and deepen it . We must actively listen to what presents itself to us, so we really know what is happening. You can guarantee the words are never what is really happening. Words are just 7 % of communication. 55 % is intuition, probably the most valuable source of information that tends to get ignored or is not noticed. People simply don't pay attention to it. When you are next in a room with someone, really notice and focus on what is happening.

Don't go in with pre-judged ideas, being so well organised that you don't improvise on what presents itself to you. This is a great habit to create and a great skill to master.

If you actively do this you will receive something so much more powerful in the relationship. You and the person in front of you will benefit. Of course, to continue this way you will need to reflect on the experience, really reflect. What was done well, what would you like to be different next time? I continue to suggest keeping a journal, making it important to you. It really is a powerful, simple tool to notice what you actually do in so many areas in your life.

Why everyone needs coaching skills

SECTION 18

targettrg.co.uk | © 2020 ClaireMoody

I felt I wanted to write a page on why it is essential for everyone to have coaching skills. I have met plenty of managers, trainers and coaches who don't understand basic coaching skills. I always feel these skills are needed to grow. People grow businesses. First of all, I often hear managers tell me how they coach their staff and then witness quite the opposite. The problem is people don't fully understand what coaching skills are. Or in fact understand the boundaries between coaching, training and mentoring.I know I have mentioned this before, but I constantly go into new sectors and the confusion is still there. It is about creating a coaching culture.

One day, you may be a manager. As a manager, you need to know all three skills and how to cross the boundaries between them. More importantly, you need to know when you are crossing the boundaries and, even more importantly, to be fully aware of what mode you are in.

For you the reader, think about your experiences. Have you been coached, managed or trained? What has really been going on? Awareness of these is so important. I love developing people's coaching skills, hence this guidebook – because everyone can grow personally. It is not a skill that is delivered by training, but coaching skills is something you can actively reflect on yourself. It is confidential, personal and real to you.

What are the boundaries between the big three? To keep it simple: a trainer teaches a skill, a mentor shares his or her own knowledges and experiences, and a coach encourages and guides. As you develop professionally in life, eventually becoming a manager, you will need all three skills and to know when to use them. Then move between them with great awareness to be fully aware of what mode you are in and how best to use which skill at which time.

Coaching skills are essential for everyone. When you have a conversation, think about it; are you judgemental in a conversation? How do you prepare for someone who is with you to open up? What triggers in you? Is the conversation based around your own learning style, your own preferences in how you communicate? I t really is important to understand " you".

This guidebook has given some great pages that are all coaching skills. I am an advocate that coaching skills grow you as a person and I wanted to share my thoughts and experiences. I am happy for you to become a burglar and take these tools and share them with everyone. Self-awareness is fantastic for growth. I do hope your journal is going well and you are actively reflecting.

There are various types of coaching, they are all useful and all work. From the solution focused coaching GROW (Goal, Reality, Options and Will) and performance coaching to Gestalt, Relational coaching. All absolutely fantastic for change.

Remember, most coaching does not mean a solution, there doesn't need to be a result. Coaching is not about offering a solution. It is about listening and thinking about what comes up, then asking permission to share what you have sensed, noticed or felt. Even with your close friends, you may notice something and still choose not to share it. This is the area that may need a change, you may need to think about something differently to work towards the core of the problem.

The onion that gets peeled back in a conversation. Practise staying non-judgemental and allow the natural process to occur. Look to guide yourself or the coachee: it's an incredible, powerful technique and can be life-changing.

There is always time in the year to make changes, it doesn't have to be January

SECTION 19

SECTION EIGHTEEN

As I write this we are well into 2020, and most of us look to make changes to our lives in January. Every year the same process takes place, but did you know that as little as 7 % of the people who want to make a change actually do make the change?

I always smile to myself as I enter the gym in January, the smile mixed with frustration. As I watch the people who have made a decision to get fit, I think, "great". I get very frustrated as the equipment is always taken, especially the treadmills. But I know by the end of the month the die- hard trainers will still be there, with the majority of new fitness fanatics gone. Why is this?

Quite frankly, people's expectations are far from realistic. Plus they want to make huge changes quickly, not really understanding that they are life changes. Sadly, that is not the way to do it. It is about little changes. Whatever you choose to do in life, whether personally or professionally, it is the little changes that benefit and start the process for the major changes to take place.

Number one, it is fantastic you have made the decision to make a change, that is a great start. A great question to ask yourself at the beginning of the year is "What do I want to be different this year?" That is the goal, then "How am I going to get there?". The key here is to break the areas down into small compartments, keeping a log of the day, what has happened compared to what you think has happened.

SECTION EIGHTEEN

You need to keep a record to follow the reality. What has changed through the day? Why? What was different about you on that day compared to another day? These are great questions and a great process to really understand where you are and to start the change process, making little changes all the time.

You are creating new habits. As difficult as it is, you have to put first what you dislike doing. If you don't, you will let things slip. You have to be disciplined but, when you are, the act of discipline in itself has tremendous benefits.

It's great to watch your personal journey, in fact it's incredible to monitor your journey. Always ask yourself, how can I make it work? Then how can you force yourself to make it work? Coaching, especially Solution Focused Coaching and GROW, work incredibly well with goal setting when done correctly, that is the key.

Finally, don't compare yourself to others. Your world is your world and every single one of us works and thinks differently. We all have different patterns, so the change is about you, as you are the most important person. So, I wish you best wishes and awesome goal setting. Go for it whether you start in February, March or September. Your New Year can start when you choose, it doesn't have to be January the 1 st.

My second guidebook is complete. Reflect and take every page as a new starter, little changes work. I would suggest using either of my reflection sheets and using your most important Journal that is personal to you. This would have started to build over both books. Write the positives and always write what you are happy and grateful for, focus on you.

Critically reflect on you, be honest with yourself. Always be YOU, not who you think you should be. Every one of us is unique and our interpretations are all different. Your world is your world, no one else' s.

Self- awareness can increase all the time; you have to actively reflect to improve this area. I have given a few areas for you to reflect on in this guidebook. I am a great believer that a short guidebook works well. A large book doesn't necessary mean you will make the changes. In our lives, short and simple is what works to move forward. Remember, small changes are the key, always working towards a goal. The goal is YOU and your personal development with some key areas from my coaching practice. There is nothing better than having exceptional self- awareness.

Remember, there has never been such a good time as now to change your mindset. Now is the time to reflect on the way you think and the way you apply yourself to any situation.

Allow yourself permission to reflect.

REFLECTION SHEET

CRITICALLY REFLECT AND YOU WILL SEE MASSIVE GROWTH

INSTRUCTIONS: This is different to the sheet you used in my first personal development pocket guide, but one that may work differently for you. You can choose either of the reflection sheets or use both. There is no right way, it is about what is right for you. So try both and see what works. Then ask yourself why one works better than the other. A good question to reflect on is am I running from the hardest reflection sheet, staying with what is easy, or am I going with the one most unnatural to me?

QUESTION #1 - Is your goal clear, challenging and specific?

QUESTION #2 - Do you work at improving something every day or week?

QUESTION #3 - How often do you pay attention to your instinct?

QUESTION #4 - Do you work at improving something every day or week?

QUESTION #5 - Are you putting yourself in situations that give you the greatest chance of believing in yourself and achieving your goals?

REFLECTION SHEET

QUESTION #6 - Do you have a plan to get there?

QUESTION #7 - Do you think and act in ways that make you feel positive and confident?

QUESTION #8 - Do you work at improving your focus on your goal? How do you do

QUESTION #9 - Do you visualise yourself interacting the way you would like to be?

QUESTION #10 - Do you imagine yourself achieving your goals? (staying

QUESTION #11 - Do you imagine yourself doing the little things that will allow you to achieve your goals?

REFLECTION SHEET

QUESTION #12 - Do you visualise positive images by acting in ways that will take you a step closer to your goals each day?

QUESTION #13 - Do you carry a perspective that centres on ongoing learning and

QUESTION #14 - Do you remain open to the creativity of the moment and the dynamics of the situation?

QUESTION #15 - Do you flow through distractions, and focus on quickly regaining control when faced with setbacks?

QUESTION #16 - Do you draw lessons, what went well, why, and what to do differently next time?

QUESTION #17 - Do you act on those lessons?

REFLECTION SHEET

QUESTION #18 - Do you re-run the things that you want to improve by correcting them in your mind? (visualisation – the power of this cannot be underestimated)

QUESTION #19 - Do you act on those reflections?

target
training associates

MEET THE AUTHOR

CLAIRE MOODY

Claire has over 35 years of experience in training and coaching and holds an MSc in executive coaching, accredited by Ashridge Business School, a world leader in executive coach training and development. Claire is a performance coach for both the RAF and the Royal Navy, specialising in Aircrew and the Air Battle Management Branch. With years of experience as a Fighter Controller in the Royal Air Force, she has significantly improved performance and pass rates for individuals undertaking challenging courses. With her executive coaching, she is extremely motivated and has a focus on unlocking life-changing insights with each coachee. Claire encourages the development of deeper self-awareness and personal insight and believes that a person's past is no indication of their future. Everyone can achieve change in whatever direction they choose, but they must decide and choose to do this, which is the key, committing themselves wholeheartedly. Claire firmly believes that people's beliefs about what is possible for themselves are their only limits. Her preference and specialisation in coaching is firstly relational coaching, which works at a psychological depth, to address deep thoughts, behaviours and feelings, and secondly performance coaching, helping individuals strive and motivate to be the best they can be. Claire is a keen runner and walker; she has always kept herself fit. She is a qualified pilot and enjoys flying in her spare time.

"It's not about being the best, it's about being the best you can be."

HAVE QUESTIONS?
Target Training Associates
107 Cheapside
London, EC2V 6DN
claire.moody@targettrg.co.uk
www.targettrg.co.uk

IT'S NOT ABOUT BEING THE BEST, IT'S ABOUT BEING THE BEST YOU CAN BE.

CLAIRE MOODY

Printed in Great Britain
by Amazon